All Scripture references taken from the KJV of the Holy Bible, unless otherwise indicated.

Seasons of Waiting: Defeating Demonic Delays by Dr. Marlene Miles

Freshwater Press 2023

ISBN: 978-1-963164-02-2

Paperback Version

Table of Contents

Seasons of Waiting

Defeating Demonic Delays

Freshwater

Freshwater Press

Waiting

What does the Word of God say about waiting? No, not the kind of waiting as a child may stare out the window anticipating a parent's return. Not the kind of waiting where what is expected will definitely happen anyway--, it's just that the child, or in some cases, a pet has no concept of time.

This book is about the type of waiting that is not going to come to pass as just a matter of time. It is about the waiting any of us may do, but something that should be ours is not happening, it is not coming to pass, it is not coming into our life. And what we need or are expecting is not coming to us for a deeper, hidden, or *spiritual* reason. How can we endure in Seasons of Waiting due to *spiritual* hindrances or delays?

Therefore the Lord waits to be gracious to you, and therefore He exalts Himself to show mercy to you. For the Lord is a God of justice; blessed are all those who wait for Him, (Isaiah 30:18).

Who likes to wait? Next to no one; we want it now. We get impatient if there is a line anywhere, such as at a restaurant. We may get restless in the doctor's reception area, or any place we have to wait. We may not like to wait for a website to load on our computer.

Do we dare tap our toes at God if He doesn't answer our prayer requests as soon as we want them answered.

The key to waiting is to consider who wants us to wait. If it's God; we trust God. Trust that He is faithful and whatever He promises He will fulfill, because nothing is impossible for God.

They say, do not pray for patience, instead, pray to the Lord for **Grace** to *wait*.

By faith Sarah herself also received strength to conceive seed, and she bore a child when she was past the age, because she judged Him faithful who had promised. (Luke 11:11)

We are waiting on whose Word, whose promise? Who said it? If God said it, we are fine, He is faithful. His Word will perform.

Some of the reasons we have to wait are on the outside of us. Demonic powers? Yes, they create real problems. Wicked people? Yes, there are evil human agents who employ demonic powers, and forces of darkness. With that dark power, if the victim is not aware and prayerful, those with demonic powers can delay, hinder, or stop your progress in life.

The good news is that intensive, prevailing prayers can break that power, terminate your wait, so you can receive the blessings the Lord has for you.

Another thing on the outside of you, are things that you didn't cause, such as generational and ancestral curses. They can also cause delays and setbacks if you don't go to the foundation to cut it off. To overcome this, you must appropriate Christ fully and get into Jesus' bloodline, else you may continue to rise and fall, never making any headway or getting the blessings you desire, need, and deserve, according to the Word of God.

These and more are causes of delays and setbacks, reasons we wait in life. As impatient as we may be sometimes, we have to wait. Having to wait could be because we don't know about the source of the delays that come upon us. Or we might know about them, but we haven't dealt with them yet. Perhaps we don't know *how* to deal with them, or we may be afraid. The Word says we have to be wise, and that the people of God perish because of a lack of knowledge.

Not Before Its Time

Sometimes there may be demonic or satanic delays, but every delay is not because of the devil. It might not be the right time or season for a thing or an event that you're asking God for--, yet. The Bible mentions the *fullness of time.*

But when the fulness of the time was come, God sent forth his Son, made of a woman, made under the law, (Gal 4:4).

Until the fulness of time, there will be Seasons of Waiting. Pregnancy comes to mind; the parents must wait to meet their precious child. We all should wait for the right time, right person, and right season to do a thing or fulfill a thing. Even in baseball –the *Batter, Batter, Batter* must wait for his *pitch.*

Waiting seasons aren't and shouldn't be seasons of doing nothing and loafing around. They can be seasons of preparation, study, travel, positioning, and in the Christian's life, seasons of prayer.

Esther was chosen by King Xerxes, but she was prepared for over a year before she was "presented" to him.

Seasons of waiting may be seasons of work: Jacob worked for Rachel for 14 years.

Jesus couldn't do any miracles until His *time* had come. In our case, when we are waiting for our "time" or our ministry to start, we should be steadfast in prayer so the anointing and Grace we need to do ministry will be afforded to us.

But sometimes it is our fault. It could be a demonic delay because of your own sin that is causing you to have to wait.

Inside You

Things on the inside of you may be the cause of your waiting, or excessive waiting. Sin invites demons or idols into your life, into your very soul, like parasites on bad meat. (Ugh, sorry).

There are several things that can cause delays and setbacks. We will mention a few.

1. **Sin**

2. **Disobedience or rebellion**

Not yielding to the will of God can cause delay in the life of a child of God and until that person conforms to the will of God, he won't move forward. Disobedience will make you have to wait and until you conform to the will of God and qualify for what He has for you, you just won't receive it.

3. Bad **attitudes**

"I don't need to repent," is a bad attitude.

The children of Israel spent 40 years on a journey that could have taken them 40 days because they didn't repent of their old way of life--, specifically their way of thinking. That is, they didn't mature in their emotions and their soul; they had unprospered souls.

God got them out of slavery, but they had to get the slavery out of themselves, *themselves*. God helps, but it is work that we must yield to. It is easier for us now under the New Covenant and with the Holy Spirit that dwells inside us. Back then, Old Testament people did not have the Holy Spirit on the inside of them, but they did have the Laws of God. God is so merciful that if we are *at least* trying,

He may be lenient with us. But doing the exact opposite of what God says to do will kindle His ire.

Even now, with salvation and the Holy Spirit, having an unprospered soul could be the reason you are still **WAITING.**

For Thought:

How would you behave if you took a trip that should take 4 hours, but it took ten times longer--, 40 hours?

How about a trip that should take 1 day, but instead it took 10 days to get there?

What if the delay was the fault of the people you are traveling with?

What if it was your own fault?

Look At Jesus

A shout out to Apostle John Brannon who always says, *Look at God.* What does a prospered soul look like? Let's look at Jesus.

1. Jesus was obedient to God, even when it was inconvenient, or it hurt.
2. Jesus honored father and mother.
3. Jesus fasted and prayed diligently.
4. Jesus resisted the devil.
5. Jesus waited for His "time" before doing His first miracle.
6. Jesus went to synagogue regularly; He grew in favor with God and man.
7. Jesus taught the Multitude and that took patience.
8. Jesus taught the Disciples separately; He was a leader.

9. Jesus stood up against what was wrong: He overturned the tables in the Temple.
10. Jesus healed everyone who asked Him; He didn't just choose certain ones and leave the others to suffer.
11. Jesus was sin-free which means He went through all the tests, trials, and temptations that man can endure, and He passed them all.
12. Jesus didn't lie.
13. Jesus didn't hoard things or try to get rich off His fame or anointing.
14. Jesus obeyed His Father, even unto the Cross, death, and Hell.
15. Jesus did all that for us. That is a hallmark of a prospered soul; they do for others, altruistically.

That's not everything, but that is a picture of soul prosperity, having control of one's emotions, will, and intellect. The only way we can be assured of prospering our souls is yielding to the Holy Spirit.

So, what are you waiting on God, *for?*

Are you waiting because you are asking God for something that you're really not ready for, or shouldn't even have? Is it that you haven't grown up, but you want all the things that grown up people get and have? Being "grown up" is evidenced in the prosperity of your soul.

You don't want to take care of grown people's **stuff**, but you want grown people's stuff. Perhaps you have the responsibility to perform disciplines such as prayer, praise, worship, read your Bible, fasting, that is the stuff of spiritual grownups. Do you do those things?

Responsibility is different from accountability, which is when you must answer for the problems that arise because of something you chose to do, or chose not to do.

If you don't perform the Christian disciplines that you are responsible to do, that could be why you're waiting on revelation or anointing from God. Because you didn't do it, you are now accountable to people and God as to why you're not ready, let's say to teach Bible Class this week.

Or **you** could be held accountable for something your ancestors did. Iniquity comes after unrepented sin. If you don't believe you sin, you will not repent, and the iniquity remains. And if your ancestors didn't repent before they left Earth, and you don't repent for them, the bloodline iniquity remains.

Ironic how something on the outside of you can create something that is inside of you. Something that your ancestors did, which is not only on the outside of you, it is also outside of **Time**, specifically *outside of your time*, since you may not have even been born yet. But that external thing can cause something that you didn't invite to be inside of you, to be *inside* you. The entities sent to enforce the unrepented for iniquities of your ancestors have a legal right to be in your life and actually inside you--, in your soul.

We all have sinned and fallen short of the glory of God. But have we repented? Do we have Godly sorrow? Has God heard and forgiven, *or* is there iniquity remaining? Iniquity that we have to endure because of our own sin, or ancestral or generational sin in our bloodline. Could that be the reason for the delay? Is this why we are in a *Season of Waiting?*

Has anyone repented down your bloodline? If no one has repented for our not-so-perfect ancestors, that could be what is obstructing our blessings and breakthroughs.

Obstructing and blocking *spirits* have permission to be in our lives when there is ancestral iniquity causing an evil foundation. We know we should have what God has promised by now, but we are still **WAITING,** because no one has repented down our family line. And, because no one has repented, ancestral iniquity is raging.

Don't Be the Sin

You need to repent. I need to repent – daily. If man is born into a sin nature, then it is natural for us to sin. We may sin when we don't think we are sinning. We may sin when we think we are not. When we are doing average, everyday things, sin may slip in. Men should always repent.

Some of the most engaging testimonies I've heard from people who say they've died and have gone to hell, or from those who say they've seen hell is the desire to come back to REPENT.

While you have life, repent. Do you even know how long it will take you to repent for the sins of your life? Repent daily.

You need to repent so you don't create stumbling blocks and obstructions in your **children's** lives – so <u>YOU</u> are not the ancestral sin that they are repenting to God for in *their* lives. Repent to God for your own ancestors, but don't <u>be</u> the ancestral sin in your children's lives. Because payment for *your* sins will be a punishment **WAITING** for your children if **you** don't repent.

Further, you can't repent on the other side of this life, so repent now. Repent today. Repent daily.

If you don't think you sin, the truth is not in you. Not repenting or thinking you don't need to repent is a bad attitude. If you don't think you should be accountable for your own actions, these are all signs of an unprospered soul.

Making a deal with the devil --, oh, you'd never do that. Let's clean this up: Making a deal with any *spiritual entity* who is not God or not *of* God will bring on the curse of the Law. Sin brings on the Curse of the Law. You are responsible or should be responsible enough NOT to do that.

If you do it and you are not accountable--, that is you do not say, *"Yeah, I did it, Lord I'm sorry, forgive me. LORD give me a repentant heart and Godly sorrow for my sins, in the Name of Jesus."* If you do not take accountability and repent, iniquity and the demons who are sent to enforce the iniquity will be WAITING for your children.

Not Ready Yet, Unprospered

Aside from generational stuff, perhaps you are still waiting, waiting on God, but God hasn't given you the thing or things you've asked for. Could be you're not ready... He told you *No*, or told you, ***Wait***.

- You're not ready for it now. God told you *No* so you can get ready.

We think *ready* means physically ready. We think we're grown enough, tall enough... we think it is how we look, how we present, or *represent*. We plan to lose 10 pounds to look nice in our new clothes. We're so busy getting our flesh ready, like we are going somewhere special, we get our hair cut, our nails done, maybe a new outfit--, but God knows what you *really* need to be ready. God looks on the inside.

We tend to look at physical readiness, because you've got company coming, you clean the house, and get food for the fridge, set the table really nice if it's a dinner party.

God cares what you look like, but He looks on the inside. What's your spirit like? What is in your soul? Not what's in your wallet, but what is in your soul?

- Pray to God: Lord, create in me a clean heart. Renew a right spirit in me.

Ask God and ask yourself: Is my soul ready to have this thing I'm asking God for? Is my soul ready to *contain* this? Is my soul ready to *do* this? Can my soul *keep* this?

This is why we need grace and patience, and strength and endurance because in the **WAITING** we are being taught, being led into an inward search of ourselves to see what we really need to do, or CHANGE to receive this asked for, prayed for *thing from God.*

In our waiting, we must keep the faith. Rehearse the Word of Promise. What did God say? Repeat it, meditate on it, rehearse that Word and keep it ever before you and get it into your spirit man. When you pray, remind God of His Word. This will help move the manifestation of His promise into your life.

Get The Fish

Jesus told two Disciples to go to the water get a fish, and it will have a coin in its mouth. These are of the Disciples who had been fishing all night one particular night and had caught *nothing--*, LISTEN: They had been **WAITING** in that boat to catch fish in their nets dropping that net down on one particular side. But Jesus came and gave a Word: *Let down your nets on the OTHER side*. With the Word from the Lord – and His presence, they got the biggest catch ever.

Later on, we see some of these same Disciples have been walking with Jesus for a while, learning, sitting at His feet, being taught--, growing in the things of the Spirit. Jesus now gives them a different instruction that will make them prosperous. Now, all they had to do is walk to the water and get a fish—they didn't even have to parlay the fish into a sale and then get the money from the buyer and then take the money to pay the taxes. See how this is different.

Is anybody getting this?

In the presence of GOD, in the presence of JESUS, by His Spirit you change. You **must** change. If you don't, then you're a Doubting Thomas, if you don't, you're a person of little or no faith. If you don't change, you are not His disciple. If you don't change in the presence of Jesus, you could be deceived, or a deceiver.

You're not like Judas, *right*?

From the first time Jesus was dealing with them --dropping the net, til now...see how the Spirit is dealing with them at this time to make them prosperous. From first meeting Jesus to now, look at how the Spirit of God deals with them, and how they function.

After sitting under His teaching for a while, and in the presence of Jesus, the disciples get a different instruction, but it is still to prosper them, but it is simpler, more direct and has fewer steps—**less WAITING**. One could say, NO WAITING, just go to the water and **get** a fish.

My take on that is GOD (Jesus) could trust them more because they had learned, they had grown, and I believe prospered in their souls.

Else, why would John in 3 John 2 be wishing that others – those who he was preaching to, would prosper unless he knew something about that, in that *his* soul had prospered? Or he had been in the company of Disciples and noticed that their souls were prospering. The seasoned Disciple/Apostle is wishing these people will receive the Word and prosper and be in health even as their souls prosper. Apostle John would not have tied those two things together unless they went together.

The **unprospered soul--,** *if* they will receive their blessings may have a longer Waiting period than a prospered soul.

We now dive deeper into this.

Benefits *for* the Flesh

Folks don't mind waiting when it is something that will benefit their flesh. *"Oh, take your time, they'll say. No rush."* I hear it at work, when someone has a chipped front tooth, they are in NO hurry whatsoever, they will even tell me they have the whole day off from work.

But when they need a small filling in a back tooth, that they think no one will see, and it doesn't hurt, and has never hurt, they will impatiently ask me, HOW long is this going to take?

How you wait is related to how bad you want it. How much do you want it? Is it fixing something that hurts or inconveniences you? Is it fixing your flesh? If it is fixing the flesh, people want that, and do not mind **WAITING** for it. That's reality, we live in a physical world with 5 senses, sight-seeing, fleshy, sight filled, a walk-by-sight world.

People will wait for what will take pain away.

In these lay a great multitude of impotent folk, of blind, halt, withered, waiting for the moving of the water. (John 5:3).

Nobody wants to hurt; if something can take pain away, make them look better, or bring them money, they'll wait. Folks will wait for an opportunity to be healed from a lamentation or limitation, or pain. They would probably never ask, *"How long is it going to take? How long is it going to take for that angel to get here and trouble this water?"*

Oh no, you don't want to irritate an angel of God that's coming to bless you. You'd gladly state, *"I've got the whole day off."* Or, *"I've got all the time in the world."*

Even when the preacher is preaching something you like, you will invariably hear someone yell, *"Take your time, pastor. Take your time!"*

Waiting in lines for the latest smart phone, toy, or tickets to a game or concert--, we'll do that. That is something for our flesh, or the flesh of whomever is getting that gift that you're going to buy.

Black Friday? We will wait at the stores at midnight because that's for our flesh. I've never seen anyone waiting in line for church. Possibly to get a good seat for a deliverance service, but your local church?

We will **WAIT** when we want something…and we will wait patiently with chairs, blankets, and food. Especially if that something we are waiting for is new, rare, discounted, or **free**.

Addicted

Then, once we get it, we want more and more of it. Appeasing the flesh is addictive.

It's why some kids don't like to go to sleep at night –they've been playing all day, and they are addicted to playing--, that's what kids do. Sleeping? Kids probably think that is wasted time; they are waiting until they can play again.

That's the same for grown folks in the streets at night, they don't want to wait to party again, so they stay up all hours--, all night to **keep** partying. Whatever is in them that is influencing this behavior just can't wait. They want more and they want it **<u>now</u>**.

Ice cream? We eat too much because we can't wait to have the experience again, so we take a bite, then another, and then another until we've had too much, or had it all… or both – all of it *and* too much. Ice cream?--, who am I kidding --, food, in general.

It is related to disbelief – no faith – Not being able to wait well--, no Grace for Waiting. We misbehave as if we don't **believe** we will have more again--, ever. We don't believe we will have this experience again and for some reason like there is no more, or we don't have the capacity to wait. This is a soul issue; that is an unprospered soul.

A prospered soul is okay with a reasonable delay, an unprospered soul wants immediate gratification. The prospered soul is fine with delayed gratification. The unprospered soul wants it NOW.

This is not to be confused with the spiritual soul who sees when a delay is unreasonable, not of God, and likely demonic.

Devil Invite

Not waiting, or not waiting well is where the devil can get into your life. It is another of his tactics. He may put up roadblocks, external or internal, to keep something from you, then make you tired, angry, irritated, by waiting. If he can make you desperate, then you may act, even if that action is just saying something stupid that invites him into your life. That's how he *gets* some folks.

Those folks who wish *thus and so*. Those folks who daydream about *thus and so*. Those folks who would *"Give anything for..."*

Deals are waiting to be made in the spirit, by evil entities, using your powerful words. You must devil proof your words. But desperation often leads to careless thoughts, and careless thoughts lead to careless words.

When you step out of faith into desperation you have left the line that you were in waiting for God and jumped into another whole lane and the line the devil has. Satan makes his line seem shorter, faster, better--, it's not. But desperation may cause people to miss obvious clues. Desperation doesn't read fine print on contracts. To be safe, do not let your flesh sign any contracts for you.

If you have a prospered soul, you may employ your soul to navigate through life and negotiate things for you, but if your soul is not prospered, trust this – your flesh will be running it.

The best set up is letting the Holy Spirit direct your human spirit; then let your spirit man navigate life, make decisions, and negotiate things for you.

Bad Relationships

People may stay in bad relationships because they want a mate so badly that they don't wait for a Kingdom spouse. They call it *settling* but we don't believe that God has anything, or anyone better or better suited for us than *that*.

Be careful of the counsel you keep. Unless you know that the person advising you is hearing from God and speaking *what thus saith the Lord*, weigh their words carefully, with a just scale. Out of the mouth flow the issues of life, but also, out of the heart the mouth will talk and talk. Lay advisers will often speak from their own experiences, successes, and disappointments. Make sure you're not listening to *"pain prophets,"* those who only speak out of their belief that life is pain and losses.

We Want to Receive

We do not like waiting on hold to handle our utility or credit card bill questions. We really don't like to wait when we have to **give** something. Oh, but if we believe we will *receive* something, we will wait, in the natural.

Well, we want to <u>receive</u> from God – so WAITING should not be an issue; it should be easy for us to wait on God, *right*? Spending time with God, in the Word, in prayer, in praise, in worship so your spirit man is built up, so your SOUL will change, grow, prosper --- that <u>IS</u> WAITING, waiting on the Lord.

We will wait for Black Friday, how about non-Black Sunday? You, too have probably heard someone saying, *"I can't go to church; it takes too long."*

Minister Unto the Lord

You know you've heard folk say that they can't go to church, or *that* church, because service takes too long.

Church is service–, it's where **you** minister unto the Lord. If you were ministering unto the Lord, which is not only your reasonable service, but also your privilege, pleasure, and great joy, you'd see things differently. It is not you *watching* others minister unto the Lord. You are not the LORD, and they are not ministering unto **you**,

Don't just sit there eyeballing everything and everyone. Plus, you don't get to judge their worship. Michal judged David's worship and she ended up barren.

Time always drags when you are not doing anything. If you are in church doing something, then time will go by quickly. Else, it will seem boring and laborious.

Furthermore: if our goal in eternity is to worship around the throne of God – that's 24/7. Do you think you'll get to Heaven, get to glory, and worship for 20 minutes and then have the rest of the day to yourself to live your best-*after*life? Your best eternity?

Of course, not.

Football Season

The average football fan during football season:

What time does church start? *How long is it going to last?*

I am not knocking football—I like football and football games. Your average football fan wants to watch football, or go to the game, but church will interfere, with the excuse that it takes too long.

Yet pregame pro football starts as early as 9:00 am and with all the ads, and the post-game, the average *televised* game lasts about three hours. If all the games and talk are done by 11:00 pm on Sunday, it's a miracle.

You will get no complaints from the person who is worshipping at the football throne; that superfan will not say that this is taking too long.

I'm not even talking about Saturday college games, Monday Night Football, and Thursday night football and the latest, Black Friday Football. Know that every time you watch, engage in, talk about football you are in service to the football throne, the football *gods*. Hermes is known as the *god* of sports. There are many *gods* of betting, and many sports fans are gamblers who are possibly as fond of betting as they are of the actual sport being played.

Three hours for one game is not too long to serve football, but a three-hour church service is not too long either--, *is it?*

Well, it depends on what God or *gods* you are serving.

This is how Baal diverts your worship that you should be giving to God in a Sunday Service to himself. Sunday is dedicated to the idol *god* of that day, the sun *god*, Ra, who is Baal, renamed.

God put you here on Earth in flesh to do certain works while you are in the flesh. If football is part of it that is between you and God. He put you here for spiritual reasons, to do your spiritual purpose and reach your spiritual destiny.

Great Waiters

There were great **WAITERS** in the Bible--, those who waited well.

David waited 10+ years to be king, while going *through*, especially with Saul who wanted to kill him.

The ones who waited the longest time: Abraham and Sarah, waited approximately 25 years for the promise: Isaac. They went through a lot in that wait, but mostly took the promise of God into their own hands and created Ishmael. So, they really didn't wait well, but God kept His Word to them. God kept covenant; God keeps covenant.

Jacob waited to marry Rachel for 14 years while working for her dad, Laban. So, he waited well.

The ones who waited the best were
Paul & Silas who sang praises
while they waited *in jail.*

Anna & Simeon waited patiently,
and in faith, for the birth of Jesus the
Messiah.

And, behold, there was a man in
Jerusalem, whose name was Simeon; and
the same man was just and devout,
waiting for the consolation of Israel: and
the Holy Ghost was upon him.

And it was revealed unto him by the Holy
Ghost, that he should not see death, before
he had seen the Lord's Christ.

And he came by the Spirit into the temple:
and when the parents brought in the child
Jesus, to do for him after the custom of the
law,

Then took he him up in his arms, and
blessed God, and said,

Lord, now lettest thou thy servant depart
in peace, according to thy word:

For mine eyes have seen thy salvation,

Which thou hast prepared before the face
of all people;

A light to lighten the Gentiles, and the
glory of thy people Israel.

And Joseph and his mother marvelled at
those things which were spoken of him.

And Simeon blessed them, and said unto
Mary his mother, Behold, this child is set
for the fall and rising again of many in
Israel; and for a sign which shall be
spoken against;

(Yea, a sword shall pierce through thy
own soul also,) that the thoughts of many
hearts may be revealed.

And there was one Anna, a prophetess,
the daughter of Phanuel, of the tribe of
Aser: she was of a great age, and had lived
with an husband seven years from her
virginity;

And she was a widow of about fourscore
and four years, which departed not from
the temple, but served God with fastings
and prayers night and day.

And she coming in that instant gave
thanks likewise unto the Lord, and spake

of him to all them that looked for
redemption in Jerusalem, (Luke 2:25-38).

Those two had waited and waited
well, to the Glory of God.

And the Lord direct your hearts into the
love of God, and into the patient waiting
for Christ, (2 Thessalonians 3:5)

We Shouldn't Always Wait

Don't get me wrong: there are times that **we shouldn't wait** --, when that wait is a delay of the enemy who wants us to miss our season, as well as divine appointments. These are more reasons to stay prayerful.

- When God says GO, we GO.
- When God says DO, we DO.
- When God says No, the answer is No.

When we get saved, the human spirit gets regenerated; God does that. The soul does not change, automatically. We must change our souls, or I'll say, allow our souls to be changed. In the case of deliverance, we must command our souls to be changed.

I command my soul to bless the Lord as in Psalm 103: Bless the LORD, O my soul: and all that is within me, bless his holy name.

The prospered soul doesn't have to command his soul to bless God; it is automatic. The prospered soul also doesn't marvel at *things and stuff*, but the unprospered soul will do just the opposite.

We don't just wait for our souls to change, we must do something; we must take action to be changed. We direct our mind, emotions and intellect; we teach those aspects of our soul. This forces our soul to prosper and come to order.

The prospered soul does not marvel at things and stuff from God, but the unprospered soul will – it is running over with emotions. self-will, disobedience, pride and any—maybe all works of the flesh.

The soul that gets things that God did not approve for them to have, that they didn't qualify for, either stole them, got them by violence or made a devil deal to go around God--because they just don't understand why God won't bless them! They will whine and complain because their souls are **unprospered.** These are **DANGEROUS** people who will lead themselves and others into peril.

Some of the *others* that they will lead into danger and hardship are their own generations--, their own children and grandchildren.

In life you are trusted with the spiritual credit card of your future generations. While you have a limited time on Earth in flesh, your bloodline lives on and on. But, if you have recklessly used, abused, and misused your children's and *children's* childrens' credit card, you've left them with a debt—a sin debt before they ever get here or are even formed in their mothers' wombs. **Don't be**

the ancestor that your generations have to repent for. Repent daily.

The prospered soul realizes there is purpose & accountability attached to everything gotten from God. What will you say when you give account to God as to how you used that gift, this gift or the other. How did you use those talents and abilities? How did you use the time God gave you? Recall King Hezekiah prayed to God and got an extra 15 years added to his life. Don't you think Hezekiah had to account to God how he used those 15 years?

How did you spend that money that God allowed you to have?

Gifts of any kind and from any source, and especially those from God should be received with decorum. Sometimes the **WAIT** is for you to grow up--, that is, mature spiritually. The waiting may be until God sees that what He gives you won't go to your head, and

He sees that you know it too. Sometimes God is waiting for us to grow up. God wants you to be aware that you are ready.

When an unprospered soul wants something, they may scorch the Earth to get it. They may choose violence, fight and struggle to get it. And then they must struggle all their lives to <u>KEEP</u> the thing they got by ungodly means. They will have to struggle to keep things that they got by ungodly means.. They may have to do ungodly things, even resorting to violence to keep things they got by ungodly means.

Sin begets sin.

Spoils of Warfare

Sometimes the thing that you get through Godly channels is a reward; it is a spoil of war, and warfare.

It's like *possessing* the land. To possess the possession, you must get rid of the enemies of God that are in it, or are claiming it. Then you go in and possess the land.

You get the land, and getting the land is part of the spoils. NOW because the enemies of God, which are your enemies too, are gone, you get to **keep** the spoils and live in peace. So, as part of your growth, sometimes the wait—the reason you are waiting is so God can see that what He gives you, you will **keep** it. You will not let the devil, his minions, or his evil human agents take it from you because you know how to war and you know how to win!!! **Amen.**

God is Waiting on You

You're waiting on God?

Nope, it's more like He is waiting on _you_.

God is SPIRIT – spirit is far faster than flesh. God is waiting on you, waiting on us.

The Lamb was slain before the foundation of the world. The answers of God are _Yes_ and _Amen_, that's why the Lamb was slain before we ever knew the Lamb needed to be sacrificed. God is far ahead of us, in **time**.

While we are yet praying, God has already answered. There is nothing that comes up in your life that God is surprised about.

God is Spirit – He is fast. Flesh is slow, folks. It seems fast to us because it's our day-to-day speed. Unless we are spending considerable time in the Spirit, the speed of flesh is basically all we know.

Those different speeds are why we must wait in faith. Without faith it is impossible to please God. Faith is like an umbilical cord that connects *us* to Spirit. If we do not connect to the Spirit of God, then our spirit man won't prosper. If our spirit man doesn't prosper, neither will our soul. Without faith, we cannot please God. A prospered soul pleases God.

We may think we are waiting on God, but really, we are waiting on *ourselves*, we are waiting on our own spiritual and soulish growth.

God, Was That You?

Waiting on God? We say that's what we are doing, but really, while God is waiting on *us*, we are waiting to **hear** God. More like we are waiting until we **hear** God, because God has already answered. We have to learn how to engage our spirit, our soul and how to sit still, we learn to be quiet, we study to be quiet so we can hear God.

Quiet the OTHER VOICES, your flesh, and the other voices in your soul because there are others and they can be chatty as they try to direct you, mislead and misguide you. If they are in your soul, in your heart, that explains why the heart of man is wicked. Not only that, the flesh cannot navigate the spirit, but the Spirit can properly guide the flesh. The flesh is the child, it's so new, relatively speaking, but it thinks it knows everything. The Spirit has been here and knows all about that; the Spirit is the parent. The Spirit should guide the human spirit.

Sometimes our waiting is waiting to hear God, but sometimes it is waiting to confirm **which voice** we just heard. We humans will say, *"God is that You? Was that You?"* because we know there is something inside of us that is doing some chatting. We are waiting to hear was that the voice that said, *More ice cream*, or the one that said, *No more ice cream.*

We have to train ourselves to stop hearing the voices of what we like.

- The voice of our flesh
- The voice of convenience
- The voice of easy
- The voice of what's in it for me…
- The voice of what will make us look good; the voice of pride.
- The voice of what will make us look good to others; more pride.

- The voice of revenge, for example.

Sometimes we may not want to hear the voice of Truth. The Holy Spirit will lead us into all Truth. We may not want to hear Truth, that voice of Truth. So we may be waiting for a *different* voice. But saints, we need to hear the voice of God and obey that Voice.

Humans often hate Truth; they can't handle the Truth. It's why they killed Prophets in the Bible; Jesus being chief among them. We need to hear Truth.

We are waiting to hear what we want to hear – this is human nature…. **Human nature is most often the thing we need deliverance from**. We are all born in sin and shaped in iniquity; we all need deliverance from that. We need deliverance from the nature of *idols* in our soul. Plain and simple, we need deliverance from human nature. What most of us would naturally do is so not God…from what God said for us to do. We need deliverance.

To Receive

We may be waiting to receive something we've prayed or asked God for. Something we need and we need it yesterday. Our spirit man waits, and if connected to the Holy Spirit, waiting should not be too difficult.

When we feel like we deserve it, we may get indignant, and that's not good.

Our soul must wait—emotions have voice, and can be screaming. Our human **will** has a voice, intellect has a voice. Intellect may be saying, *This doesn't make any sense to do this or that. It doesn't make sense to do nothing right now.* We're waiting, but it doesn't make sense to the intellect which is filled with man-made knowledge.

The will may be yelling to try to make you take the solution into your own hands. Sarah and Abraham made Ishmael.

Emotions may be frazzled, and falling apart, screaming, *"I don't know if I can handle this another moment!"*

Our flesh hates waiting the most. Flesh knows it has a limited amount of time. The spirit will live on, but the flesh has a limited time and wants it **now**.

When the body hurts, yeah, waiting is tough. When the body is in pain, waiting is so hard. When the mind and soul hurt – yes, that's difficult too.

If we are unprospered or serving unprospered demons – and they are all unprospered, when they insist on humans taking on their nature, most behavior will be a combination of evil and childish. Unprospered souls, and the demons running those souls want immediate gratification.

Flesh wants it now: all demons want it now, that is a clue that It's not you, it's what is *in* you: *pride* wants it now. *lust* wants it now. *Jealousy* and *revenge* both want it now. All works of the flesh want it now. These are clues.

Bodily functions sometimes cannot wait and should not wait. Depending on one's endocrine system, hunger shouldn't always wait. Cold is something you feel to save your life, maybe that shouldn't wait either. Driving tired for example is the same as driving while intoxicated, experts say; many times, sleep shouldn't wait. Needing the facilities – the restroom--, it's not good to hold it. Those things are not demons, but they may need the ***now*** kind of attention.

We know the works of the flesh, pride, lust, revenge, greed, and et cetera are demons that insist on their own way, and they insist on it now. Don't give in to them. Resist the devil and he will flee.

The Devil Waits

The devil is especially busy because he knows his time is short in the scheme of eternity. But at the same time the devil will **wait** strategically. He will wait to pounce.

Demonic *spirits* will hide, they can hide in a person until the appointed time to ambush or take someone by surprise. Some diseases, for example, are already in people by the age of 2 years -- but may **wait** to express themselves. For example, by two years old all of us have a certain virus but it may not show up in our lives until we are older or undergo a particular stress. And, that's another reason to stay prayed up.

Spirit is Fast

Time & **Waiting** have an interesting relationship in the spirit. If you have faith, you already believe you receive it, therefore until it manifests in the natural, you do not even feel like you are waiting, because **YOU ALREADY HAVE IT**, because you have faith and you believe God.

Having faith, real faith circumvents the feelings of waiting. If two agree as touching – that means two agree on a thing and behave as though they are already touching that thing—it is already manifested in the natural, they shall have that thing. So if you receive it in the spirit, then you *have it* much faster.

Spirit is fast – God created the Earth and world in 6 days. Here's a hammer and nails – you do that.

You can't.

Jesus said if they tear down this temple, He will build it back up in 3 days – of course, He meant resurrected, and not actually build anything, but the SPIRIT is fast, it creates very quickly.

Spirit only takes as long as it takes for you to imagine a thing. You already have it, depending on your faith; sometimes you don't even have to say it – you already have it.

Now, after you believe and believe you receive it in the spirit, there's another layer of waiting – you must, in faith, wait for it to manifest in the Earth.

Waiting With Other People

Some have no grace; if another is waiting, they just *have* to be in front of others who are also waiting, in lines, in traffic, in life.

I was in New York, there were three of us in our party waiting at a posh hotel for the best buffet--, like ever, to open for dinner. We went there early, on purpose. There was no one else in the queue; we couldn't believe our good luck. It was an hour to opening time. After 15 minutes of waiting, a woman about 50 and her two daughters, in their 20's, with some type of Eastern accent came to the line and got in front of me and said, We were here first. Now, I was with my husband and his son – two grown men who said nothing when I looked at them.

Would we argue about being first in a line to a restaurant where all the food is already prepared on a buffet, and it seats 120 people? Of course not. Without arguing we let her stand ahead of us. I said to the mother of that group, *"There is plenty good food for all."* I said that thinking we might strike up a conversation about that prime rib on the buffet.

Instead, she rolled eyes of hate at me. She didn't accost either of the men that I was with; just me.

Why?

I don't know.

The line grew, there were about 60 people waiting; that restaurant is very popular. It was time; now the host began to take groups of ten to the elevator to go up to the buffet. The rude lady and her two ducklings were in front and rushed to the elevator, where they got on first and stood in the back. We knew, because we had been there many times before, that first on the elevator puts you in the back of the line when you reach the *maître d'* on the restaurant level.

Yes, we got off the elevator first and retained our first in line position. We were seated, went up to the buffet, got our delicious food and sat down to eat. We noticed them seated not too many tables away with no food or anything, because they obviously didn't know how this worked.

What was all that drama for?

The devil.

He that is first will be last, and he that is last will be first.

Wait well, my friends.

Yeah, New York, again. Somehow, we badly timed a trip to New York and arrived there during the Macy's Day

Parade. The streets of Manhattan were a mad house. The cab let us off with our luggage and we were making our way through the crowd. We needed to cross 6th Avenue, but the parade was going past.

Policemen were there because lots of people needed to cross the street. We found a line of others who also wanted to cross, and got in that line.

I looked up and couldn't believe how huge those character balloons are and how high they are in the air from the ground, like 30 feet or more.

A tiny woman, about 50 years old approached me in the line and said, *I've been here since 5am to get this spot and you're standing in front of me, I can't see.*

I looked at her and pointed to a 30 ft tall Woody Woodpecker balloon, at least 30 ft in the air, and said, *You can't see that?* I think I said it twice for emphasis. Of course, there were street level floats, but there was no way I was blocking her view, we were at least 12 people deep from the parade route.

This little woman wanted to insist. My husband, of course, said nothing. Then I gently broke it to her that we were all in the line to cross the street. I asked her if she was also crossing the street and if not, why was she in this line?

Don't get me wrong, I like New York City. We should pray for those who ignorantly and without resistance let the devil use them for evil.

Wait well, my friends.

- Lord, give us Grace to **WAIT** when we should wait, but help us grow and prosper in our spirit man and in our souls while we wait, so we can be in health and prosper even as our souls prosper. Teach us, like the sons of Issachar, to know the times. Amen.

Sometimes you are just to *occupy while you wait,* sometimes work while we wait, as Jacob did to marry Rachel. Attacking other humans, for no apparent reason is not waiting well, nor is it soul prosperity.

We should all wait for the right time, we wait for our pitch, our chance; we wait for the *fullness of time.*

You want to go fast? Get in the Spirit. Lord, teach us to *occupy* so we are not complacent and sitting around doing nothing in life, while blaming it on waiting.

- I bind the *spirit of laziness,* in the Name of Jesus.
- Lord, don't let us just sit and observe the clouds, else we will never plant.
- If we are Soldiers waiting… ready and waiting for Your command, You are the Captain of the Host of the Army of the Lord. Lord, lead

us into victory and give us the spoils, in the Name of Jesus.

If you are one who is waiting, continue doing what God said. Behave yourself the way Jesus would. Don't let those who want to pick a fight because they are not good at waiting pull you into anger or confrontation.

Anger is probably the number one thing that the devil uses to divert your blessings from you. Peace draws prosperity; anger pushes it away.

Waiting In Captivity

Sometimes we are stuck, waiting in captivity –, waiting and praying for a jail break, waiting for deliverance.

- **Lord don't let us WAIT our lives away.**

Like Paul & Silas if we are to praise our way out of captivity, LORD let us praise! Holy Spirit help us; let everything within me praise the Lord. Bless the Lord, O my soul and all that is within me.

Give us Grace, that we wait well Lord when we should wait. Amen. Let us wait with anticipation –and in faith versus waiting in disbelief or in dread, or not waiting at all, but falling for devil deals, or making Ishmaels.

Our ability to wait changes as we grow in the Lord. As we get used to how the Lord operates, we learn to trust Him. As we get used to good things coming to us, we learn how to wait on the Lord even better and we wait with Grace.

Our souls prosper.

The more good things we experience in Life, the better behaved we are. For instance, when you can have a certain food ever so often you behave differently than if you think you'll never have it again. Because of proper exposure to experiences, we don't wait like wild things, trying to consume all of it -- like we've never seen food, or whatever we are having, as though we are going to have the last of this.

Waiting *for* Others

Soon we stop wanting things to heap on our lusts and we become servants and helpers to one another. Jesus did; He came to serve us. What did Jesus come here and amass for Himself on Earth? Nothing. He didn't try to make a name or fame for Himself. No fancy Ivy League college education. No expensive sports cars. No mansions here on Earth. No 401K or Golden Parachute, No luxury vacations. He came to serve.

Anna and Simeon waited on the Lord, waiting on the consolation of Israel. We will have much in Heaven--, rather than chasing the Earth version of what is above. That is delayed gratification--, soul prosperity.

Discipleship Changes Your Soul

Relationship and discipleship with God should change us. It changes you and it changes what you wait for, how you wait, and what you do and how you behave as you wait. Discipleship changes your soul; it grows us up and gives us soul prosperity. We wait by sitting at the feet of Jesus; as we learn we become changed.

It's not your relationship that changes in the sense that you're tighter with God now, or God owes you because you went to church and missed the first football game of the three that play on Sundays – all season. Even though you did that, that doesn't mean that now you are tight with God, and He owes you. It is not *quid pro quo* with God, and you're entitled. It's not that.

It's by relationship but it is by much more than relationship – you've changed. Your soul has grown, our souls have prospered. Jesus is the same yesterday, today, forever. We are the canvases that must change because we were born in sin and shaped in iniquity.

That is why what's in us that is not of God., it has to go! Whatever we picked up on the way to where we are now, if it is not the Holy Spirit, it has to GO!

Whatever picked us up and we like it, and it is entertaining our flesh, it has to GO! The more we entertain it the bigger the flesh gets.

All of this is deliverance and it is us changing, prospering us in the things of God. We are becoming more filled with the Holy Spirit. That is deliverance. That is us building up our spirit man, possessing our souls in sanctification and honor, prospering our souls. We are being changed.

Now when the Lord says I have this for you, He might mean right now, or tomorrow, instead of 10, 15, or 25 years from now. Just go get a fish and there will be a coin in its mouth.

Faint Not

In the process of waiting, the devil comes against you with so much that you may get weary of waiting and stop believing, in faith, for the promise that God gave you. Don't do that. You may faint and give up in the process and go create your own Ishmael. Don't do that.

You've changed in the things you ask God for. First you may have asked for things to heap on your own flesh, or so your neighbors can see your new car--, to bump up your pride.

But now you ask God for right things, things that are for your life and godliness that have purpose and will not hurt you or anyone else.

Whereas before, you may have asked God for anything that came to mind:

a Ferrari, a Lamborghini, -- God's got all that and can get all that, but what would be the purpose in your having it? To please your flesh?

Now, because of time in the Word, His presence and prayer life, your soul has prospered, and you can ask for something knowing the answer is *Yes* and *Amen* and you may only have to wait a short amount of time and it will manifest in your life.

By now you know and God knows that you are *so* ready, and that your faith is so strong, God may just place that blessing in your hands today or tomorrow… ask God.

For the purpose of warning – there are millions who came out of Egypt who did not make it into the Promised Land – they died without ever having seen the promise (Hebrews), but they waited. They waited the worst, poorly, continuing to sin, murmuring, complaining, idolatry, sex sins—

Was any of this soul prosperity? No, it was not. They were delivered from the bondage of slavery, but their minds had to be changed, so their actions would be different.

> Beloved I pray that you would prosper and be in health even as your soul prospers. (3John2)

The Wilderness Israelites in their Wilderness Mentalities **died** without ever reaching the Promised Land. They died in faith, without receiving the promise. This shows that you can have faith for a thing, but _how_ you wait is very important. It can help get you into that promise or keep you out of it.

The Wilderness generations went into the Promised Land, but the former slaves did not. These all died in faith, not having received the promises, but having seen them afar off, and were persuaded of *them*, and embraced *them*. They saw it, they knew it, they had faith for it, but didn't possess the land. They got weary.

They fainted, and started the murmuring, complaining, sinning… they *died*. Don't do that.

When you come out of sin, stay out of sin. Murmuring and complaining is evidence of having NO GRACE to WAIT.

Your momma is in the kitchen cooking dinner, you're at the table, you can smell it, but for some reason you don't think you will eat, ever again. So, you start whining and complaining--, this is the sign of a child; we have to grow up. This lack of self-control and soul prosperity is how Esau lost his birthright by trading it for food from Jacob.

God is the Ancient of Days; how old are you in your *relationship* with God? By your behavior, at the dinner table, for instance, how old do you think God would say you are emotionally? In your soul? How old does your spirit man behave?

What might *you* be at risk of losing or trading because of lack of soul prosperity?

How to Prosper in your Soul

We have already looked at Jesus as a model of soul prosperity. Do we think Jesus was born that way? Jesus was all man. He was touched with the feelings of our infirmities, and that surely would include defects and flaws of the soul. If you look back on Jesus' human side, you will see all kinds of *issues* down His bloodline.

Jesus had to prosper in His own soul, else why was he in the Wilderness fasting? Why was He turning down temptations from the devil? Temptations are there to have a man trade his soul for whatever is offered. Instead, Jesus chose to keep his soul, maintain it with sanctification and honor. At the end, Jesus said, *"The prince of this world has nothing in Me."*

Demons, devils enter the soul of a man to influence and ruin him. They create a purchase point for more devil leverage against that man. We should be like Jesus and able to say the same.

Hereafter I will not talk much with you: for the prince of this world cometh, and hath nothing in me, (John 14:30).

We must do all we can in order to prosper in our souls, including reading and listening to the Word, because faith comes by hearing. Fasting. Praying. Take deliverance in difficult situations. There are some very stubborn curses and demonic covenants that only deliverance can cancel and break.

Do the above steps first, you will get levels of deliverance, but when things seem resistant, seek a deliverance minister. The habits that you began before seeking the deliverance minister will make deliverance easier for you. This proves that what you do while you wait (wait for a deliverance minister) will make a difference in whether you get one, and how easy or difficult it will be to get your deliverance.

Also, Godly disciplines will help you **keep** your deliverance, because you will need to keep it. The demons that oppressed you will want to come back and keep controlling and ruining your life.

Therefore the Lord waits to be gracious to you, and therefore He exalts Himself to show mercy to you. For the Lord is a God of justice; blessed are all those who wait for Him, (Isaiah 30:18)

Blessed you are in your service to God and for **waiting** on God, not going ahead into danger, destruction, or disaster.

God will wait and see that your soul is prospered, then He will show Himself when he knows you are ready and that you can maintain and keep the possessions you possess, you can keep the land He's given you. Maintain the territory that you've gained for the Kingdom, and properly enjoy and hold onto the spoils of your warfare. God needs to know that you can do all this while keeping the devil out by not making devil deals and giving in to temptations.

Prayers Against Delay

Repent. Forgive me for my sins, Lord, and the sins of my ancestors going back before Adam and Eve, where I retrieve my glory and my essence, in the Name of Jesus.

Holy Spirit Fire, fall. Fall on these prayers in the Name of Jesus.

In the Name of Jesus, I break evil covenants and curses.

By the power of Your Spirit, Lord, heal my faulty foundation, in Jesus' Name.

Every problem that I brought into my life through sin that is causing me delay and setback, Father, cleanse and deliver me, in the Name of Jesus.

Anything in me that is blocking the blessings promised in the Word of God from coming to me, come out of me now, in the Name of Jesus.

Every breakthrough-delaying power, every breakthrough-prolonging power, DIE, in Jesus' Name.

Fire of the Most High, consume every *spirit of delay* and *setback*, in the Name of Jesus.

I break every evil covenant and curse that allows the *spirit of delay* in my life, in Jesus' Name.

I bind every strongman delegated to hinder my progress or steal my blessings. Lord, I ask Mighty warrior angels of God to remove them from the gates of my blessings, in the Name of Jesus.

Lift up ye heads, all ye Gates and the King of Glory shall come in. The King of

Glory, strong and mighty in battle. There I will recover all my virtues, gifts, talents, abilities, breakthroughs, and blessings, in the Name of Jesus.

Every demonic agent sent from the pit of hell to cause delay and setback for me and my family, fall down and die, in the Name of Jesus.

Every satanic power controlling my finances, causing me not to enjoy the fruit of my labor, die by Fire, in the Name of Jesus.

Any curse operating in my life causing marital delay to my Kingdom spouse, receive the consuming Fire of the Holy Ghost, and die, in Jesus' Name.

Every enchantment from the enemy to cause delay and setback in any area of my life, I render you useless, powerless, weaponless, by the power in the Blood of Jesus.

Every divination organized by the devil and his cohorts against my life, die, in the Name of Jesus.

Anybody born of a woman who has hindered my blessing, I command you now, in the Name of Jesus, release my blessings, by the power of God.

Lord Jesus, bring favor into my life right now, in the Name of Jesus.

Any *spirit* or power that is blocking the prosperity of my soul, I command you to leave my soul, leave my life, and **die**, in the Name of Jesus. (X2)

I break every barrier that is blocking me from arriving at my breakthrough, in the Name of Jesus.

Every curse that I have brought into my life through disobedience and ignorance, break by Fire.
Break by Fire (X3), in Jesus' Name.

Every *spirit*, power, or evil entity that I have let into my soul that is now demanding worship, and that I take on their nature, I bind them with fetters that have locks and no keys. I command them to come up and out, up and out...I send them to the Abyss where there is no water and no return, in the Name of Jesus.

I decree that every demonic hole, pit, or trap the enemy has prepared for me, let them fall into their holes, pits, and traps, by the power of the Holy Ghost.

Household witchcraft, stand down. (X 3), or receive the wrath of God, in the Name of Jesus.

Every mountain on my way to victory, be removed by the Fire of the Holy Ghost, in the Name of Jesus.

I set myself loose from every satanic bondage, in the Name of Jesus

Every curse by anyone living or dead that has been pronounced against my life and destiny, break by Fire, Break by Fire, in the Name of Jesus.

I break every evil covenant allowing the curse, in the Name of Jesus.

I bind and cast out every demon or devil sent to enforce the curse, in the Name of Jesus.

I break the bondage and the yoke that results from the evil covenant and curse, by the power in the Blood of Jesus.

Any power preventing good things from entering my life, be destroyed, in the Name of Jesus.

Anything in me preventing good things from entering my life, be destroyed, in the Name of Jesus.

I come against every *spirit of fear, anxiety* and *discouragement*, in the Name of Jesus.

Every false *god*, every idol demanding worship, come out of my life now, in the Name of Jesus.

Fire of God, locate my foundation, and destroy every generational curse working against my life, in the Name of Jesus.

Thank You, Lord for the Word tells us that we are to prosper and be in health as our soul prospers.

For our emotions. Lord, touch our emotions today; restore our souls, in Jesus' Name.

For our intellect, Lord, give us the Mind of Christ, with Wisdom, Understanding, knowledge, and a rational brain.

Give us a God-focused view so our souls will prosper, keeping our minds stayed on You.

Every *spirit of retaliation* because of this message or these prayers, backfire 7X, in the Name of Jesus.

I seal these declarations across every realm, era, age, dimension, and timeline, past, present, and future, to infinity. I seal them with the Holy Spirit of Promise and the Blood of the Lamb of God, in the Name of Jesus.

Amen.

Dear Reader:

Thank you for acquiring and reading this work.

May the Grace to wait when you should wait be upon you. May you move through life from Grace to Grace, strength to strength, and Faith to Faith.

I pray the Fire of the Holy Ghost be upon your life to destroy everything that would cause you to have to wait when you should not have to wait.

Above all, may your soul prosper day by day, moment by moment, so you can say, like Jesus that the prince of this world has nothing in Me.

The promises of God are Yes, and Amen. Let that be your case as you abide in Him and He abides in you. In Jesus' Name, **Amen.**

Dr. Marlene Miles

Recommended: **Living for the Now of God** https://a.co/d/h6b8bA3 Soul Prosperity, Your Health and Your Money https://a.co/d/2pqwJUG

Art adapted from Dreamstime.com

Other books by this author

AK: The Adventures of the Agape Kid

AMONG SOME THIEVES

Ancestral Powers

Barrenness (Prayers Against)

Blindsided: *Has the Old Man Bewitched You?*

https://a.co/d/5O2fLLR

BEST SELLER! **Courtroom Prayers at Midnight** https://a.co/d/OSOLA3E

Churchzilla, The Wanna-Be, Supposed-to-be Bride of Christ

Demons Hate Questions

Devil Weapons: Unforgiveness, Bitterness,…

https://a.co/d/iGyHeLr

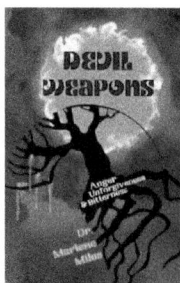

Dream Defilement

Don't Refuse Me, Lord (4 book series)

Every Evil Bird

Evil Touch

Fantasy Spirit Spouse

FAT Demons (The): *Breaking Demonic Curses*

The Fold (5 book series)

>The Fold (Book 1)

>Name Your Seed (Book 2)

>The Poor Attitudes of Money (3)

>Do Not Orphan Your Seed (4)

>For the Sake of the Gospel (5)

Fruit of the Womb (Barrenness, Book 2)

https://a.co/d/chR6FIO

got HEALING? Verses for Life

got LOVE? Verses for Life

got HOPE? Verses for Life

got money?

How to Dental Assist

How to Dental Assit2: Be Productive, Not Wasteful

Let Me Have A Dollar's Worth

Level the Playing Field
https://a.co/d/1BdoVWA

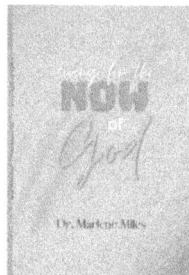

Living for the NOW of God

https://a.co/d/gHjvntR

Lose My Location
https://a.co/d/crD6mV9

Man Safari, *The*

Marriage Ed. Rules of Engagement & Marriage

Made Perfect in Love

Motherboard (The)~ soul prosperity series

Plantation Souls

Power Money: Nine Times the Tithe

The Power of Wealth *(forthcoming)*

Rules of Engagement & Marriage

Seasons of Grief https://a.co/d/gIrFD7U

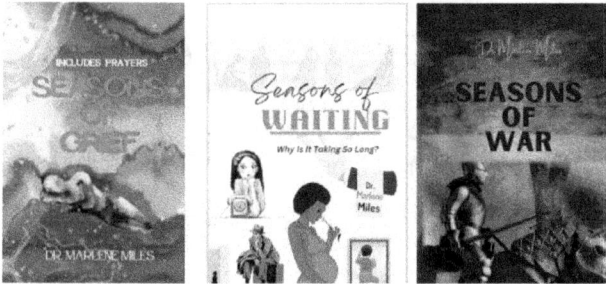

Seasons of Waiting

Seasons of War https://a.co/d/adKy3y9

Soul Prosperity soul prosperity series 3

https://a.co/d/5p8YvCN

Souls Captivity soul prosperity series 2

The Spirit of Poverty

This Is NOT That: How to Keep Demons from Coming At You

Throne of Grace: Courtroom Prayer

Time Is of the Essence

Too Many Wives: *Why You Have Lady Problems*

Tormenting Spirits
https://a.co/d/dAogEJf

Triangular Power *(series)*

Powers Above

SUNBLOCK

Do Not Swear by the Moon

STARSTRUCK

Uncontested Doom

Upgrade: How to Get Out of Survival Mode

Toxic Souls (Book 2 of series)

Legacy (Book 3 of series)

Warfare Prayer Against Beauty Curses

Warfare Prayer Against Poverty

What Have You to Declare?

When the Devourer is Rebuked

The Wilderness Romance *(series)*

- *The Social Wilderness*
- *The Sexual Wilderness*
- *The Spiritual Wilderness*